The Let's Talk Library™

Let's Talk About
Needing Extra Help at School

Susan Kent

The Rosen Publishing Group's
PowerKids Press™
New York

For Jeffrey—Tricia, Danny, and Jon   —S.K.

Thanks to the students and faculty of the Hastings Elementary School   —F.E.

Published in 2000 by The Rosen Publishing Group, Inc.
29 East 21st Street, New York, NY 10010

First Edition

Book design: Erin McKenna

Photo Illustrations by Felicity Erwin

Kent, Susan, 1942—
     Let's talk about needing extra help in school / by Susan Kent.
          p.   cm. — (The let's talk library)
     Includes index.
     Summary: Discusses some of the reasons children may need help in school and how to get the help they need.
     ISBN 0-8239-5422-6 (lb : alk. paper)
     1. Learning disabled children—Education (Primary)—Juvenile literature. 2. Learning disabilities—Juvenile literature. 3. Learning—Juvenile literature. [1. Learning disabilities. 2. Learning.] I. Title. II. Title: Let us talk about needing extra help in school. III. Series.
LC4704.73.K45 1999
371.9'0472—dc21   99-12550
                                                                                               CIP
                                                                                               AC

Manufactured in the United States of America

Table of Contents

Kristy

Kristy is having trouble learning math. She feels bad. Everyone else seems to understand the math lesson. Why doesn't she?

Her teacher suggests she stay after school for some extra help. Kristy doesn't want her classmates to find out and make fun of her. Her teacher is nice and keeps it between them. Working alone with her teacher, Kristy catches on. She is happy that she is starting to understand her math lesson, and she feels good about herself again.

◀ *Kristy gets the extra help she needs in math class and now she feels better about herself.*

Needing Extra Help

In school, some things are harder to learn or understand than others. You might be good at addition and subtraction, but find it hard to multiply or divide. You might be great at reading, but not spelling. You might enjoy a subject like social studies, but have trouble catching on to some of the ideas.

It is okay to need extra help. It can even be fun! You get extra attention paid just to you.

Lots of kids in school need extra help. Different kids need help with different things. Everyone learns in their own way. ▶

Why You Need Extra Help

There are many reasons for needing extra help. You may have trouble with letters or numbers. Maybe **b**, **d**, **p**, and **q** all look alike to you. In math, you may put numbers in the wrong place or reverse them. You may not remember your math facts or what the teacher tells you to do. You may not understand new words or ideas. Maybe you find it hard to pay attention, sit still, or get **organized**. If you have these problems, you are still smart. You just need some extra help.

◀ *Some students get extra help in small groups.*

When You Need Extra Help

You know you need extra help when you have tried your best but still don't understand a subject. Poor grades might mean you didn't study hard enough or pay enough attention. They can also be a sign that you need some extra help.

When something is not clear to you, ask your teacher to explain it in a different way. It is important to **admit** you need extra help. If you get help, you can stay on top of your schoolwork and not fall behind.

This girl gets extra help from her teacher so she can do her social studies homework. ▶

Giving Yourself Extra Help

If you are tired or hungry, you cannot do well in school. Be sure to give yourself extra help by getting a good night's sleep and eating a healthy breakfast. That will help you to stay **alert** and to **concentrate** all morning, until lunchtime!

You can also help yourself in class by looking at your teacher when he or she is talking. Nod your head or smile to let the teacher know when you understand. Raise your hand if you have a question or would like to hear something repeated.

◀ *These students have questions so they raise their hands to let their teacher know.*

13

Getting Extra Help from Others

Tell your teacher, parents, or guidance counselor when you need extra help. Let them know that you have tried hard to understand, but still don't get it. They will be glad to help you.

At your school, your teachers and counselors can give you special tests that show the subjects you need extra help in. They also have tests to figure out your learning style. These kinds of tests don't have grades and can be fun to take.

Special tests help show your teachers the best ways to help you learn. ▶

Learning Styles

Everyone learns in different ways. You might learn by doing something once, or it might take you many tries. You might learn best when you hear things read aloud. You may need to look at pictures or charts to help you learn. Touching objects can help you remember shapes. Activities like field trips or putting on a play can help you if you learn best by doing things.

It is important to get the right kind of help for the way you learn best.

◀ *Some students, like these, enjoy learning by using tape recorders and earphones.*

We Learn in Different Ways

The way you learn, your **abilities** and your problems, can sometimes be **inherited**, just like the way you look. You may have green eyes like your mother and red hair like your Aunt Mary. You may be good at sports and so is your Uncle Joe. If you are good at music, your grandmother may be a singer. If you have trouble paying attention or sitting still, maybe your father did when he was young, too.

The way you learn is just one part of a very special person—you!

This girl loves to study science, just like her mom did when she was in school. ▶

Kinds of Extra Help

Sometimes your classroom teacher gives you extra help. She might give you more time to finish your work or tap your shoulder to remind you to pay attention. A **tutor** or special teacher can also give you help. This teacher may work just with you or with a small group of students. You do different things than you do in your regular class. You might practice words or letters using flash cards or by saying them into a tape recorder.

It feels good when you get the extra help you need.

◄ *This girl plays a spelling game with her tutor. She is getting extra help and having fun!*

Doug, Katie, and Juan

Doug, Katie, and Juan meet with their tutor, Mr. Cole, each morning in the **resource room**. This room has extra supplies to help them learn to become better readers. They use special books and computers to learn new **vocabulary** words. They have enough time to practice using the words until they really understand them. The computers talk to them and tell them when they are doing a good job.

Doug, Katie, and Juan have fun while they learn to read.

Glossary

ability (uh-BIL-uh-tee) A skill or talent.

admit (ad-MIT) To bring something out into the open by talking about it.

alert (uh-LERT) To be wide-awake.

concentrate (KON-sen-trayt) To pay very close attention.

inherited (in-HEHR-ih-ted) Passed down from family members.

organized (OR-guh-nyzd) To keep things neat and in order.

resource room (REE-sors ROOM) A room in a school where students get extra help with the subjects they find hard to understand.

tutor (TOO-ter) A teacher who works with one or a few students outside the classroom to help them learn.

vocabulary (voh-kab-yoo-LEHR-ee) A list of words, usually in alphabetical order, with their meanings.

Index